CONTENTS

Active Listening — iii
Introduction — v

1. Communication Techniques — 1
2. How to Improve Your Listening Skills — 17
3. 6 Tips for Active Listening — 31
4. Improve Your Listening Skills with Active Listening — 44
5. How to Make Someone Remember You for a Lifetime — 57

Afterword — 71

ACTIVE LISTENING

Improve Your Conversation Skills, Learn Effective Communication Techniques, Achieve Successful Relationships with 6 Essential Guidelines

Joseph Sorensen

Copyright 2019 by Joseph Sorensen - All rights reserved.

This eBook is provided with the sole purpose of providing relevant information on a specific topic for which every reasonable effort has been made to ensure that it is both accurate and reasonable. Nevertheless, by purchasing this eBook, you consent to the fact that the author, as well as the publisher, are in no way experts on the topics contained herein, regardless of any claims as such that may be made within. As such, any suggestions or recommendations that are made within are done so purely for entertainment value. It is recommended that you always consult a professional prior to undertaking any of the advice or techniques discussed within.

This is a legally binding declaration that is considered both valid and fair by both the Committee of Publishers Association and the American Bar Association and should be considered as legally binding within the United States.

The reproduction, transmission, and duplication of any of the content found herein, including any specific or extended information will be done as an illegal act regardless of the end form the information ultimately takes. This includes copied versions of the work, both physical, digital, and audio unless express consent of the publisher is provided beforehand. Any additional rights reserved.

Furthermore, the information that can be found within the pages described forthwith shall be considered both accurate and truthful when it comes to the recounting of facts. As such, any use, correct or incorrect, of the provided information will render the publisher free of responsibility as to the actions taken outside of their direct purview. Regardless, there are zero scenarios where the original author or the publisher can be deemed liable in any fashion for any damages or hardships that may result from any of the information discussed herein.

Additionally, the information in the following pages is intended only for informational purposes and should thus be thought of as universal. As befitting its nature, it is presented without assurance regarding its prolonged validity or interim quality. Trademarks that are mentioned are done without written consent and can in no way be considered an endorsement from the trademark holder.

INTRODUCTION

The book will help in learning how to become an active listener via easy to follow tips that can be incorporated in one's daily life. In the book, one will find discussions on various techniques of communication.

One will then learn practical skills on how to improve listening skills, which work in scenarios where communication involves one-on-one interactions or groups. The listening skills discussed involve both those that need one to speak and those that can be achieved without any verbal action.

The book contains practical tips that assist in developing the skill of active listening. It contains examples of how the tips can be used in varied situations. One will find examples of which tips to consider first depending on the scenario one is faced with at any one time.

Going through the book, one will find ways in which they can improve their listening skills, through the process of active listening. Details on how one can measure the improvement in the skill of listening are shared. Pitfalls that should be avoided in the journey of sharpening listening skills are also found within the book.

Finally, the book shares ways in which one can use the skills learned in listening in making themselves memorable for a lifetime. Varied scenarios and examples are shared that one can implement comfortably in one's journey to build better and stronger relationships that are fulfilling.

COMMUNICATION TECHNIQUES

Communication techniques, by definition, are ways in which communication concepts are practically applied. Communication occurs in three main ways:

- Verbally
- Non-verbally
- Via written word
- Visual

In regards to verbal communication, the same can take place in person or via varied media e.g., through a telephone conversation. The applications are relevant even in unexpected situations that one comes across in their daily lives. The techniques used are varied and should be applied in the context of what one faces at any given time. The communication techniques that are effective are simple and easy to incorporate. The techniques are applicable even in the world of the written word. The advantage that the written word has is that the information to be passed can be edited until a version one is comfortable to transmit is arrived at. This gives one an opportunity to deal with mistakes in advance. The foundation of developing effective communication skills is first focusing on the sharpening of the skill of listening, active listening. Active listening is about both hearing what message is being transmitted and understanding the message.

In a world where everyone's attention is drawn by a myriad of issues, communication techniques are one way of helping one stand out from the crowd. Being unique in this aspect is of importance both at the workplace, particularly in scenarios requiring teamwork, and within one's social circles. In professions that are sales-oriented, effective communication techniques can be what makes the difference between being a professional success or a failure. Those within industries dealing with resolving conflicts are aware of how critical active listening as the foundation of effective communication is. Effectively communicating allows one to end up with a majority of win-win scenarios. It should be noted though that some situations require one to turn off the technique of listening.

Effective communication techniques can be considered as a tool of persuasion. When using communication techniques to persuade, one should consider the setting within which the communication will occur as a factor that can affect the success of the overall goal. One should remember that sometimes persuasion can take time. Communication techniques used can determine the message quality received. Anyone concerned about effective communication does not assume that it has taken place but instead focuses on ways to improve and confirm that indeed, communication has occurred effectively. Going through the communication techniques, one will learn how to help the other party receive communication as intended by the sender of the message.

When looking at communication, it is important to take into account how cultural context affects the process. To understand the importance of the techniques of communication, one needs to look at the process from the point at which its effectiveness can be affected.

Communication can face challenges from the point of origin, during transmission or at the point of receipt.

In a lot of scenarios, quite a number of people who are by all standards considered smart assume they are effective communication-wise whilst in reality, this is far from the truth. This lack of effectiveness can affect one, even in public speaking scenarios. The key focus from the speaker's point of view should be to deliver the intended message in a way that the one on the receiving end is able to understand it.

The focus in regards to communication techniques is for one to remember that small changes make a huge difference in the end result. Not taking into account, e.g., a letter in a word can make a huge difference; in the end, the result would be a problem in communication. Some of the things that are important to consider in regards to the techniques of communication include:

- Approach
- Attitude
- Practice

Working on communication techniques in advance proves helpful in scenarios where one has had no time to prepare on what to say. These techniques are particularly effective in high-pressure situations. Several people struggle to communicate with others in such scenarios where one is in an unfamiliar environment.

An example of an unfamiliar environment that one could take advantage of communication techniques is in the art of cold calling. Cold calling is a skill whose effectiveness makes a difference in work situations requiring its use for e.g., for those within the sales environment. For common everyday situations like answering a random question from someone, this skill, too, comes into play. Working on these techniques make a difference in everyday life as humans are generally exposed more to spontaneous situations of communication as compared to planned occurrences, the former exemplified in everyday introductions to people one meets for the first time.

Another everyday unplanned scenario, particularly in the workplace and business situations, is the process of feedback. The techniques help in receiving feedback from those whom one can ask for their opinion on certain issues of interest to them. How one reacts to feedback can be determined by how one communicates. This is particularly critical in scenarios when dealing with e.g., an employee that one does not want to lose. There are individuals who consider whether to stay or leave a workplace based on the work environment. The work environment is affected by how communication takes place.

On the flip side, the communication skills of workers can have a direct effect on how well a business does perform at any given time. Those who have attended seminars and/or conferences are familiar with question and answer sessions where communication techniques come into play within a spontaneous context. Communication techniques can also be used by students to aid in learning. One needs to understand that communication flows dually in terms of direction. One must also be aware that individuals generally can become good or better at communication if they chose to incorporate the techniques.

Though one may face challenges in communicating, the techniques can help one overcome the obstacles. The goal should be not to entertain preconceived ideas of what one's audience will think of their communication.

It is important to consider anxiety as one of the factors that may affect how effective communication does take place. Effective communication can also be affected by communication etiquette. To tackle different aspects of communication techniques it may be useful to categorize the same from the point of dealing with factors that may affect how effective one is in communicating i.e., finding out how to deal with anxiety and communication etiquette. The communication techniques that will be discussed are applicable to both adults and children. Adults can utilize techniques to help children improve their communication. The techniques will also assist in helping one engage in small talk.

Managing Anxiety

It is said that a large majority of people, even those who have experience speaking publicly, suffer from some sort of anxiety when in a situation where they have to speak to people. Some individuals describe this feeling as one of nervousness or in extreme cases, stage fright. Some compare the experience to one of being terrified. One should aim not to let fear interfere with their overall goal of communication. The overall way to overcome this fear is to push past it. It is important, though, to realize that in many cases, this feeling may be adequately managed.

There are techniques that can be used to manage this kind of anxiety. Some draw from this feeling, turning it from the point of weakness to one of strength by using it as a tool to sharpen their focus. Anxiety exhibited by a speaker from the audience's perspective can result in making the audience uncomfortable. It is upon the one initiating the communication to make the audience comfortable. Making the target audience comfortable allows them to be in a position of receipt as opposed to a position of disengagement. Anxiety can occur at the point just before one starts the process of communication.

Some common signs of the anxiety include shaking, and sweating, or what some describe as having butterflies in their stomach. What follows this is an inner voice where one confirms to themselves the feeling of anxiety they are feeling through unspoken words. As one continues this thought pattern, one may feel as though their audience has arrived at a similar conclusion in regard to their feelings of anxiety. If this process continues, one ends up increasing the tempo of their feelings of anxiety.

Tools that can be used to deal with anxiety include:

- *Acknowledgment*: the first one needs to acknowledge that the feeling of anxiety is present. At this point, one needs to remember that the feelings they are experiencing are normal for the majority of individuals, that the reaction is normal. Using this line of thinking can help one stop their thoughts of anxiety, going beyond the point of control. One may still feel anxious yet have it under control.
- *Re-framing*: This technique involves changing one's perspective on how one considers how the communication process needs to look like from the viewpoint of the target audience. The challenge here is to change one's mindset from looking at the communication process as one that has to be perfect. When one aims for the process to be perfect, one ends up focusing on the mistakes that can occur or that are already taking place. This line of thinking ends up

making the speaker more nervous. One should always remember that there is no perfect way of communication. The best way to deal with this is to look at the process as a means of conversation.

To make the communication process conversational, one can use the following tools:

- **Questions***:* Using questions at the beginning of communication, turns the process into one that is interactive as it pulls in the audience by giving the target audience an opportunity to contribute. The questions that encourage contribution are open-ended in nature. The open-ended questions can be used as a communication technique that allows one to gain insight into the motivation behind their dialogue partner. Here, one can make use of all kinds of questions, including rhetorical ones. The closed-ended types come in handy when one is looking for concise answers.
- **Conversational language***:* The speaker can use language that brings them closer to the audience as opposed to one that pulls them away from their target audience. Here, the definition of language should be thought of in the context of both verbal and non-verbal types. A non-verbal language that is considered to be anti-conversational includes placing of hands across the chest or even moving away from an audience physically. Non-verbal language can also be referred to as body language. To take control, one should be intentional about their non-verbal language. To be believable, there should be a sync between verbal and non-verbal language. The speaker should use language that the audience can relate with, and that speaks to their scenarios. The focus here should be on achieving a state whereby the audience gets a feeling of being included. This can be achieved simply by using pronouns. Examples of pronouns include the words I, she, and us.

- *Time orientation:* In this technique of managing anxiety, one should focus on being alive to the present moment that one finds themselves in, as opposed to worrying about the future. Being in a future state here means, for example, wondering if the audience will find one funny. Not focusing on what would happen can make one less nervous. A way in which some speakers use to keep their mind on present circumstances include:
- *Physical activity*: The act itself of being physically active forces one's mind to focus on the present situation that they are currently faced with. Physical activity here can include taking a walk before the speaking session.
- *Music*: one can choose to listen to music that has a calming effect on themselves.
- *Tongue twisters*: these have been shown to help speakers focus on the present as one's mind will focus on trying not to say out the tongue twister wrong. The twisters have the added benefit of helping one warm their voice.
- *Filler words:* Examples of filler words include uh, so and like. The use of filler words, particularly as the one speaking, may give the message that one is uncertain of what they are saying. When one projects uncertainty in the context of communication, one loses the opportunity to be considered as trustworthy by the recipient of the message. This becomes critical in scenarios that require the persuasion of the other party, e.g. in sales processes. One should avoid using these words even in the context of filling a pause whilst speaking. It would help to know that it is quite a common occurrence for those who speak.
- *Speaker notes:* To ease one's anxiety when speaking, one can choose to have notes that give a general outlay of what they are looking to talk about. The notes can be in the form of a question format so that it helps drives on speaking from a conversational point of view. The conversation can help in reducing the stress that causes anxiety. Speaker notes can

also help in a professional setting e.g., when holding meetings.
- **Research**: One can manage anxiety by carrying out investigations on the audience or person they are going to communicate with. This may make one be at ease as one would have confidence in the type of person or audience they are going to interact with.

Communication Rules

Taking advantage of communication rules is another major way of dealing with obstacles that can rise up against effective communication, and can help one feel comfortable handling speaking situations. The communication rules can be considered as forms of improvisation. The focal points that should be considered here are:

- **Silence**: Skilled communicators are able to draw on the effect of silence to cause individuals to speak of topics they would otherwise not be ready to discuss. The trick here is not to give in to the temptation of filling up pauses of silence with words. One should instead use this tool to pull in their partner in communication into taking part in the conversation. This tool can allow one to gather detailed information as the communication partner looks at filling in the silent pauses. The focus should be on one to achieve a state of attentive silence.
- **Mirroring**: This technique is one that involves copying the gestures and stances of the one they are communicating with. The effect that this has on one's communication partner is that the other party gets a feeling of being comfortable, as it seems as though the communicator is reaching out to them. This should be done subtly; otherwise, it will lose its intended effect. The technique is a great tool that has a positive effect, particularly when handling conversations that may be considered as being difficult. When not in one location, mirroring can be looked

at as responding using the same media as one's dialogue partner.
- *Flexibility:* This tool is to be looked at from the viewpoint where one is the listening partner in a communication process. Here, one should be able to read through what is not being communicated through spoken words. This is considered as active listening.
- *Feedback:* Requesting feedback or giving feedback is a tool that can be used to achieve effective communication. The tool allows for those involved in the dialogue to feel that they are an important element of the process.
- *Curiosity:* A successful communication tool that one can use is building up one's curiosity in those whom they are in communication with. This, from the viewpoint of the other party, is perceived as having a genuine interest in who they are and/or the situations they find themselves in. The originator of the communication also gets to gain respect in the eyes of the recipient of the communicated message. An added advantage to this tool is one is able to understand the reasons why the other party does what it does. Once the other party feels understood, it is then easier to persuade them. When one gets to understand the reasoning behind the actions of another party, an opportunity to create stronger relationships with them may arise. This tool also helps the originator of communication to appear less intimidating.
- *Ourselves:* Here, one aims to be perfect or right in the communication process. The more one tries to aim for perfection, the more likely one is to make a mistake. One's personality can affect how well we can be at communicating in a given scenario. Individuals who have a personality skewed towards planning, in a bid to communicate well, may end up doing it wrong as they may end up stressed about what could go wrong as opposed to being relaxed. This will lead to ineffective communication. The trick here is not to over-plan ahead and to forget

oneself in the context of spontaneous communication scenarios.

The focus here should be on just communicating in tandem with the situation that is unfolding. One way of forgetting oneself is by encouraging one's partner in communication to be the one to speak more. When one finds a way to move out of being the center of the focus of communication, one gains the trust of the other party in the communication process.

Another scenario is when one's personality causes them to follow certain patterns in the communication process. The patterns followed sometimes are of no benefit, and may even be detrimental to the communication objective. These patterns occur due to muscle memory. The way to suppress these patterns is by forcing oneself to develop new ways of communicating, particularly in the context of spontaneous scenarios. What works well in spontaneous occurrences for one to seem to communicate genuinely, is to respond to unfolding events as they occur as opposed to reacting based on preplanned thought processes, the latter of which will come off as one not being authentic from the point of view of the recipient of the communication.

- *Viewpoint:* This is about how one views the communication situation one is faced with. One can view it as either an opportunity or a challenge. Looking at it as an opportunity is about having a positive mindset whilst looking at the situation as a challenge is embracing a negative mindset. How one approaches a situation will determine how effective one is at communicating with the communication partner. This is because our viewpoint determines how one feels, and therefore, generally, how one will act and speak. One should aim to view communication scenarios as opportunities. Seeing the unfolding scenarios as opportunities allows one to relax and even have fun while at it. This can be considered as a type of re-framing. A negative mindset may cause an originator of

communication to seem to be critical, which may lead the recipient to build a wall of defense around them, making the communication process ineffective.
- **Enthusiasm***:* One's moods can have an effect on how the recipients in a communication process perceive a message. It is, therefore, imperative for one to aim to communicate with enthusiasm, taking into account the overall context of the message they intend to pass. When one is engaging, the message communicated can be considered from the viewpoint of the recipient of the message as being one that is engaging. When a communication process is considered to be enthusiastic, the recipients are more likely to exhibit a positive response.
- **Listening***:* This requires the speaker to slow down to avoid answering what one thinks their target audience is asking without actually waiting for the audience to complete having their say. One should come from the point of view that they are there to serve their audience. Listening, therefore, becomes a way for the speaker to understand exactly what the audience requires. Slowing down requires the speaker to pause between the words they speak. Listening helps the speaker to also tap to the strength of being in the moment. The speaker should, therefore, respond only after listening to the audience. This will allow the speaker to tailor a response that is appropriate for the audience.

Working on the listening part of communication can help one get others on to their side. One should consider that listening should focus on both the verbal and non-verbal aspects. When one listens, the other party feels as though the listener has put their interests before his or her own.

- **Story Telling***:* Responding is best done within the context of a story. As much as it is best to respond via storytelling, it is important to remember that the story should be structured.

The structure helps one have a better chance of speaking successfully. The structure will help the intended audience process the information from the speaker more effectively. The use of structure helps one remember better and helps the speaker not lose the attention of the intended audience. The structure also helps in detailing expectations to the audience. Some of the structures that are useful in speaking situations are:

- *Opportunity-Answer-Advantage Structure:* In this story structure, the speaker first talks about an available opportunity, followed by an answer for such an opportunity, and then the advantages of providing answers for the opportunity that has been presented. Following this structure allows the speaker to be persuasive.
- *What-Why-What Structure:* This allows answering the questions of what something is followed by why one should consider it and lastly what is to be done going forward. This structure makes sense in scenarios where questions are to be answered or where introductions are to be made. In the latter case, the initial section of the structure is turned into who.
- *Humor*: this is a tool that can be used to connect in various scenarios. The challenge with this tool is the perception of the dialogue partner, whether what is portrayed as humor is considers to be funny or not. What is funny to one person may be offensive to another, particularly within the context of culture. Humor can be used to bring practicality in communication. The tool can be useful when handling tense scenarios, e.g., when communicating correction. In such scenarios, its effect is that it can negate the possibility of communication being perceived as offensive.
- *Approval:* A number of individuals crave for approval. The need for approval can, therefore, be used as a communication technique. When one shows approval to the one they are communicating with, a bond between them is created. The one who receives approval tends to feel

heard and understood. This can be done by stating to one's dialogue partner what it is about them or their situation that one admires—approval when genuine can be a tool of persuasion.
- *Eye contact:* Here, one needs to consider the cultural context of the communication process. In some scenarios, eye contact may make one's dialogue partner uncomfortable or may even be interpreted as being offensive. On the other hand, avoiding eye contact may be construed as one lacking confidence. One should try and achieve a comfortable balance, as too much eye contact may be construed as a form of intimidation. The goal here is for one to use eye contact to communicate interest in the person and topic being communicated whilst ensuring both parties are comfortable. From the originator of the communication, eye contact is a tool that is used to keep the focus of the recipients of the message.
- *Vulnerability:* Sharing one's struggles is a communication technique that allows for a connection with one's dialogue partners. Vulnerability within the communication context builds trust, which is an ingredient for building relationships.
- *Conciseness:* To be effective in communication, the goal should be to pass the message across in as few words as is practical. When communication involves an overload of words or information, attention can be lost. Also, a speaker may be considered as being boring, which is a risk of losing a connection with the dialogue partners. Lack of conciseness also leads to loss of clarity regarding the message intended to be passed. When there is too much information, one runs the risk of the intended recipient being unable to process the given message. Questions can be used as a way of giving a break for long conversations.
- *Teamwork:* When communicating, it is best, depending on the context of the communication, to make the recipients of the message feel as though the one speaking is on their side.

When one builds this similarity in focus with the intended recipients, a bond is created. Here, one should consider using words that signify teamwork. Such words include 'our,' 'us,' and 'we.'

- **Empathy:** One of the communication rules to follow is to try and put oneself in the situation or mindset of the one being communicated with. This makes the other party feel understood and of value. Empathy can be used as a prediction tool in terms of the reactions to be expected from the message or how a message is passed across. The goal here is to match how a message is delivered to the personality of the intended recipient.
- **Name:** Depending on the cultural context, using a person's name whilst communicating to them can make one feel valued, appreciated, and recognized. Using one's name to address them also draws their attention to the conversation. Here, it is critical to remember that pronunciation should be correct in the name.
- **Equalization:** When communicating, it is helpful in some situations to create a sense of lack of superiority. This helps in making a recipient feel valued. The recipient in return would feel that the originator of the message can be trusted.

The above communication rules help a speaker to determine how to say something. The speaker, therefore, is only left with the task of deciding what they are going to say.

Utilizing the tools on how to manage anxiety and to communicate allows one to be a more effective speaker as one continues to use the tools to practice speaking. The techniques allow one to be a speaker who can connect to audiences. One can also use the tools to appear assertive, to be understood, and as a point of influence. The tools may mean the difference between plateauing professionally or moving to the highest attainable level in one's chosen career path. Those with great communication skills are able to express themselves well in interviews. Those looking to attract investors to their dream can use the techniques to aid their goal. Professionally, the techniques can assist one in their quest to request for a raise.

One should always remember to be adept at using communication skills. Focus should be on one as a speaker and as a listener.

Additionally, some skills may be tailored to particular kinds of audiences or dialogue partners. Some of these audiences include:

- *Hostile Audiences:* When communicating with a hostile audience, one should remember to acknowledge the emotions of the audience whilst not going ahead to name the specific emotion. Naming the emotion can lead to heated discussions on whether or not the emotion has been identified correctly. This does not, in most cases, augur well with audiences. Once the emotions have been acknowledged, the speaker can then reframe the question asked to a viewpoint that they are more at ease with, in terms of responding to. It is important for a speaker dealing with hostile audiences to develop the skill of being aware of the environment they are to find themselves in.

This means that one should try as much as possible to ensure that they do not get caught unaware by such scenarios. This gives leeway to the speaker to respond effectively. If the speaker goes into defensive mode in hostile scenarios, they will unfortunately not be able to listen to the audience.

- *Remote Audiences:* For this type of audience, it is important to use engagement techniques that would make them involved in the communication process. Some of the engagement techniques include:
- Use of imaginary situations: The speaker should engage the audience in a language that causes them to develop a picture in mind.
- Use of polling techniques: This can be used to allow remote audiences to get involved in ongoing communication.

- Use of collaborative tools: Tools such as Google docs can be used to engage during the communication process actively.

For remote audiences, the main focus should be making communication varied and engaging to allow for a genuine connection with the speaker.

- ***Intercultural Audiences***: The speaker who communicates with intercultural audiences should find out what challenges speaking to intercultural audiences come with, and if possible preplan on how to deal with those challenges with the overall aim of being able to navigate the challenges to connect with the audience. The speaker should find out what the expectations of the audience are within their cultural context. This can be as simple as taking into consideration the type of dressing. The speaker should be aware of the rules and regulations that govern the culture of the audience they are to come in contact with.

HOW TO IMPROVE YOUR LISTENING SKILLS

Listening is a skill that is critical to the success of the effectiveness of the process of communication. Its importance is heightened in the current context of human interaction where technology has, over time, become a challenge in achieving effective communication. This is particularly true where technology is considered as a distraction. The underlying focus when it comes to improving listening skills is to be patient and to focus on becoming an active listener. Active listening can be defined as listening with full attention. Active listening can also be referred to as a conscious type of listening as it starts with one making a conscious choice to listen actively. With active listening, one overtime gets to see the improvement that is sustainable and predictable. What makes the skill of listening essential is that it is in essence, one giving up a resource they can never take back i.e., the resource of time. Active listening is considered as a psychological tool.

In a world that is highly competitive, the skill of listening can be a tool used to put one or an organization in the leadership position. Leadership that listens is considered as one that is responsive and understanding. This is because when used correctly, listening can improve how accurate an organization or person is in providing value. When an organization adds value, they, in turn, can gain loyalty from their customers, which can mean an increase in business opportunities presented to the organization. Listening well in itself is a tool that can be used to save time by reducing the amount of error likely to occur due to misinterpretation.

The skill of listening is applicable in varied scenarios, including at work and within the context of personal life. The advantages of listening include:

- Having the ability to make one feel heard either as a speaker or an audience. This can be useful in scenarios involving conflict or for effective selling.
- Using the skill to build relationships that are strong.
- Being able to build genuine connections with others.
- Being able to learn new languages.

When one feels heard, one is more likely to express their genuine viewpoint on a myriad of issues. In an environment that requires teamwork, good listening skills are critical in bringing team members into sync. This creates a work environment where solutions and creativity easily flow. Creating a positive work environment via the use of listening skills can mean the difference between retaining good workers and losing them to the competition.

Listening skills can assist individuals in letting go of emotions that are negative in nature. This is exemplified as utilized by counselors during counseling sessions. There are particular skills that one can use in order to listen effectively. These include:

Attention: Part of being a good listener is giving speaker attention by focusing fully on the speaker. This will involve looking at the speaker and watching for cues that are non-verbal in nature that is also referred to as body language. Somebody language cues are placing hands across the chest. The tone of a speaker's voice is also an example of a non-verbal cue. A speaker's tone can give a good listener a glimpse of the emotional state of the speaker. When one does not focus on the speaker, one will miss these cues. Non-verbal cues can give a listener insight into the emotional state of the one speaking. One can try to repeat the words a speaker uses internally in one's head as a means of keeping the focus on a speaker. The act of such repetition allows one to reinforce the message that the speaker is trying to get across.

When giving speaker attention, be sure to do so with balance, so that the speaker does not interpret the attention as staring or intimidation. Also, one should try to individualize the attention specific to the emotions of the speaker. To be a listener who gets the whole picture of the message being transmitted, one must process both the verbal and non-verbal in tandem. Depending on where communication is taking place, the listener might have to mentally get rid of any sort of distractions e.g., background activity. Distractions can be internal or external. Internal ones include one's thought pattern moving away from what a speaker is saying.

It is also important to individualize the type of attention to give as what may be considered as attention in one set e.g., eye contact may be considered rude in another culture. Giving cues to show one is attentive is more important than the type of cue.

Avoid deflection: Deflection can be defined as pushing back or away from. In the context of developing effective listening skills, it is exemplified when a listener makes the decision to move the topic of conversation from the one the speaker is currently on, to one that is of interest to them. This may be due to the listener being uncomfortable or even bored with the topic at hand. It would be more subtle to use close-ended questions to shorten the message of the speaker than to change the topic outrightly. The skill to be developed here is to subtly encourage the speaker to move away from the topic at hand without taking over the process of doing so.

From the speaker's point of view, a listener who chooses to deflect comes off as one who has no respect for them or even one who is selfish.

Avoid outsmarting: To become a good listener, one must refrain from taking the focus from the speaker to themselves. One of the ways one does this is by choosing to share a scenario where one faced the same situation as the one that the speaker is trying to share. This portrays the listener as one who is boastful and selfish.

Avoid setting judgments: This involves one holding back from being critical of the one they are listening to. This way, one gives themselves a chance to see a situation from the viewpoint of the speaker. In some scenarios, using this tool to improve listening may end up allowing an unexpected connection to occur between the most unlikely of people, even as they take note of the similarities between them. One should avoid voicing criticisms while listening as the speaker may decide to stop communicating. Generally, when one entertains critical thoughts as they are listening, the same shows up via non-verbal cues e.g., through frowning. The non-verbal negative cues can cause the speaker to become defensive, leading to ineffective communication.

Not judging can also help one not to come up with preconceived conclusions that may change the perception of what the message was intended to be. Passing judgments can also be in the form of mentally correcting one's accent or spelling. Doing so distracts one from forming the habit of effective listening.

Big picture: When listening to a speaker, one should aim to focus on the overall message as opposed to the details, as the latter may lead to unnecessary distractions that lead one to miss out on what was the focus of the message that the speaker wanted the listener to get. In a one-on-one setting, allowing distractions may force the one listening to ask a speaker to repeat themselves. This may cause the speaker to feel frustrated and may portray the listener as one who is disinterested in the message being passed. Unnecessary repetitions due to the lack of focus on the side of the listener are also time-wasting.

When one focuses on the big picture, they may also be less critical, therefore becoming more effective at listening. When one is less critical, one focuses on the content shared in communication as opposed to mistakes perceived as having occurred.

Context: To be an effective listener, one must always put into view the context within which a message is being transmitted. The same message can have varied meanings in different contexts.

Culture: Effective listeners are culturally aware. One being culturally aware allows for one to use tools for effective listening within a cultural context productively. Being unaware of culture may inhibit effective communication. This is because what one culture considers appropriate, another may consider insulting.

Emotions: Connecting with the emotions that a speaker displays or is feeling makes one a great listener. Doing so can allow the listener to be empathetic to the speaker. In some cases, it can lead to the building of a successful relationship between the speaker and the listener. This relationship can then be leveraged for other situations. The speaker will be able to tell when a listener connects to them emotionally, via the mirroring of emotions that will take place via non-verbal cues on the part of the listener. For one to identify with the emotions of a speaker, one has to have their full attention on the speaker, which in turn makes one a better listener as they are actively listening.

One way a good listener connects with a speaker is by amplifying the emotions that the speaker displays.

Facing: Depending on the cultural context, it is advisable to face one in whom one is in communication with. This implies interest, confidence, and in some scenarios, respect. It also gives the speaker the indication or go-ahead to start or continue communicating. Looking away from the speaker may signify the opposite. When facing one speaking, be sure to get rid of distractions. What one should remember when using the tool of facing to become an effective listener is that they are to do this without portraying a confrontational posture.

Feedback: To be a good listener, one must learn the art of giving feedback. Feedback can be given either verbally or non-verbally. Generally, the non-verbal aspect makes up the bigger composition of communication. I am giving feedback signals to the speaker that one is attentive and interested in the message being transmitted. Giving feedback also helps a listener stay attentive. In the context of feedback, the listener should aim to mirror the feelings of the one they are listening to. Feedback can be in the form of paraphrasing, which helps in ensuring the listener and the one speaking are on the same page. Paraphrasing is also a way through which the listener demonstrates to the speaker how well they can listen.

Giving feedback can also help to avoid misunderstandings, which if not dealt with, would lead to ineffective communication. Feedback can also be a way through which a listener can communicate to a speaker that they have understood the message transmitted. One should be aware though, that the feedback given should portray that one is listening yet not necessarily that they are in agreement with the message being transmitted. The feedback should focus on acknowledgment as opposed to the agreement unless the listener actually agrees with the message being communicated. When giving non-verbal feedback, the listener should use one that is comfortable to them, yet take into account the cultural context of where the communication is occurring. This is to ensure that they don't look or feel awkward or portray a message to the speaker that is varied from their intended communication.

Giving feedback may also reduce on time wastage, as the one speaking may not feel the need to repeat their message, as a way of being sure that the one listening has understood the message that the speaker had intended to communicate. When giving feedback verbally, a good listener should not repeat word for word what the speaker says, but instead, rephrase the message communicated. The focus here is to give feedback on the listener's own words. It is also important for a good listener to give feedback at the appropriate time. The appropriate time is dependent on the context within which the communication is occurring. One can sometimes tell that it is an appropriate time to share feedback by studying the cues given by the speaker. Some cues here can include the speaker pausing or looking at the listener for evidence that they are being heard.

Another point to consider when giving feedback is that the response should fully be about the speaker. A good listener will not include themselves in the feedback by e.g., using words that would be inclusive of them like the word we. When using rephrasing for feedback, it is best for the ownership of the rephrase to be the listener. The rule of thumb in regards to feedback, though the context should be considered, is that it should be shorter than the message received from the speaker.

To avoid being critical in the context of feedback, one should aim not to let their own value systems and biases block their ability to listen actively.

Goal: To be effective at listening, one should come up with a practical goal for the same. A goal in listening effectively can be that one will only speak a quarter of the time and listen to the rest of the time that the communication process is taking place. The use of this tool, though, it must be applied in the context of how and where the communication process occurs. The overall goal generally would be to speak less and listen more.

Growth: A way of becoming a good listener is to consider listening as an opportunity for growth. Humans have had different experiences in life, can be a source of learning if only one truly listens. Having a growth viewpoint in the context of listening will be portrayed even in your non-verbal or body language positively. The growth viewpoint may also give one information on how to deal with issues in a different manner. Listening can be an aid in the journey of personal growth or self-development.

Hear: To be an effective listener, one should always put themselves in a position to actually hear what the speaker is communicating. This may mean adjusting the volume or requesting that the speaker increase how loud they are speaking. It may also mean the listener needs to get rid of distractions or even draw closer in proximity to where the speaker is. If at all the listening part is being affected by something that needs medical attention, one should aim to seek for help if possible in order to become effective at listening.

Interrupt minimally: Interrupting an individual as they speak may lead to them getting frustrated. They end up with the feeling of not being understood nor heard and even disrespected. These feelings can lead to obstacles against effective communication occurring. Depending on the context, the speaker may decide to stop communicating. The speaker may interpret the interruption as a show of rudeness, which may end up destroying a relationship. Also, an interruption can be in the form of trying to predict verbally what the other party is trying to say. This has a presumption that the listener can read in advance the thoughts and feelings of the speaker.

Doing so can lead to a myriad of misunderstandings. It may also project to the one speaking that the listener is impatient. Interruptions give a feeling of a contest where two parties are competing for who should be heard. This does not augur well with the goal of building relationships through active listening. To avoid being a source of interruption to one speaking one can choose to:

- Practice having one's mouth stay shut during listening. When an individual chooses to focus on keeping their mouth closed, they can end up becoming better at listening.
- Take notes of what one considers to be important points raised by the speaker. Also, one can put down points that one considers of importance that come to mind as they listen to the one speaking. The other party may consider it a sign of respect when someone puts down what they are saying as it means that it is important to the listener. It should be noted though, that some speakers interpret this action as evidence of the listener being distracted, and may, therefore, discourage it.
- Change where one's attention is at. This is about placing attention on the aspect of listening as opposed to the one of speaking or responding as the case might be. One can also choose to come up with a goal to talk less than they speak at any given time.

Another challenge with interrupting that should be considered is that it can cause the speaker to forget what they were talking about in the first place. If the speaker cannot remember what they were talking about, the conversation which may have been of benefit to the listener is cut off prematurely—interrupting one while speaking can also be considered as time-wasting. Interruption can also lead one to not fully understanding the message that the speaker is looking to pass. In order not to interrupt, one should believe that they will not forget any questions they would want to ask when it is now appropriate to do so.

Mirroring: To be a good listener, one needs to practice reflecting the speaker. The reflection should cover the emotions, gestures, and even posture of the speaker. Mirroring can be extended to the language being used. The trick here is to reflect in a subtle manner so that the same does not come off as weird or off-putting. If not subtle, the speaker may consider the listener as one who is making light of their message. The reason why this tool of listening is to be done subtly is that its effect functions at the subconscious level. When done well, a bond is created subconsciously between the speaker and the listener.

Multi-Tasking: Though in some circles, multi-tasking is considered a valuable skill, it can become a distraction in the process of learning to be an effective listener. This is because one's concentration will be split among varied activities or tasks. From a listener's point of view, it means one will not be able to give full attention to the speaker, which in turn will lead to ineffective communication. Depending on the context, multi-tasking while listening may be considered as disinterest or rudeness from the point of the speaker. The less one multi-tasks, the higher the focus one has on the activity they are pursuing at the moment, even listening.

Notes: A listening tool that can be utilized depending on the context within which communication occurs is the use of notes. Writing down general ideas of what one gets in a message can help solidify one's understanding of what one is communicating. The speaker can also translate writing notes to mean interest in their communication. In some instances, though, some may consider it a distraction. Writing notes encourages one to be active while listening. It also helps one keep track of the flow of the communication being disseminated. Active listening as exemplified by the writing down of notes makes the process of listening productive.

Writing notes lessens the possibility of such information being easily forgotten. Writing notes can also help a listener ignore distractions in the environment. Some of the distractions that writing of notes can sort is the feeling by the listener, that if they do not speak at once, whatever they wanted to ask or say will be forgotten by the time it is now appropriate for them to speak.

Not offering solutions: When listening to someone describe a challenge they are facing, quite a number of people feel the need to offer solutions. The reality though is that many are just looking for a listening ear. For a win-win situation, one can use the skill of listening, which involves probing using questions to help without offering solutions. Offering direct solutions may come off as impatience, where one wants the conversation over and done with. Using the right questions can help the speaker arrive at their own solutions while leaving with a feeling of having been heard and even understood.

Patience: To be a good listener, one must learn to be patient. This one tool will help in not giving in to the urge to interrupt, and helps one focus on getting the message being passed. One should remember that skills take time to develop. The tool of patience also helps one stay the course of being consistent in practicing listening. Learning to be patient also helps an effective listener focus on not letting their mind be distracted from the communication currently taking place.

Pause power: As a listener, one should wait for when a speaker pauses to request for clarification as opposed to interrupting the one speaking midway through their speech. Doing so may portray to the speaker that they are respected and are being listened to. It also shows a speaker that the listener is interested in what they have to say. If one has nothing to say during a pause, the listener should not say anything, no matter how uncomfortable it gets.

Posture: To signify interest, a listener should adopt a posture that says they are ready to listen to the message of the speaker, a posture that portrays the listener as one who is approachable. One should be careful not to adopt a defensive posture in a context that requires the speaker to be relaxed. Posture is basically about how one sits or stands. When one leans forward, it signifies interest with the opposite signifying disinterest.

Practice: To improve one's listening skills, it is good to find a way to practice consistently the tools that lead to their improvement. One way that one can practice their listening skills is by listening to children. The younger a child, the more likely they are to communicate via non-verbal cues. Practicing listening skills with children can help one sharpen their skills of reading between the lines or interpreting non-verbal cues well. The advantage of practicing with children, too is that they are generally brutally honest.

Present: To be a good listener, one needs to aim not to lose track of what the speaker is saying. Doing so can be interpreted by the speaker as being disinterested and rude. In some cases, the speaker may completely stop talking. One should aim to be fully present. It is advisable, if important, to request the speaker for time to sort out whatever may be distracting one from fully being present for the speaker. Once the distraction is sorted, being a good listener requires one to give full attention to the speaker.

Questioning: Questions can be used as a means of becoming a better listener. The focus here on questioning should be the bid to understand better the one speaking. One should avoid asking questions that have no correlation with the subject that the speaker is focused on, as it portrays disinterest in the matter that is of interest to the speaker. If one finds themselves having made such a mistake, they should then use questions that take the speaker back to the subject that was originally of interest to the speaker. The type of questions used will also determine how well of a listener one is.

To gather more information, open-ended questions are preferable. When looking for concise responses, a listener may opt to use close-ended questions, which are questions whose response would be a yes or a no or that give specific answers that do not allow for further elaboration. It should be noted that close-ended questions may portray a listener as one who is disinterested in what the speaker has to say. The listener should aim only to ask questions once a speaker finishes a point they are looking to pass across. When asking questions, it is important to remember that the questions should not be for expressing counter-arguments. Questions that begin with the word why can cause a speaker to go into a defensive mode. Questions that begin with either the words what or how are preferable.

Refocusing: Any time one finds themselves drifting away from the message being transmitted, the listener should mentally redirect themselves to what is being said so as to be a good listener.

Self-awareness: To be a good listener, one must endeavor to work on their level of self-awareness. In the context of becoming a good and effective listener, this can mean being aware of the level to which one feels the need to talk. How much does one feel the need to be heard as opposed to giving others the gift of being heard? Being aware of one's challenges can help in determining which areas to work on first that maybe the rate-limiting factor in one's journey to becoming an effective listener. The essence of being self-aware when it comes to developing effective listening skills is to focus on quieting down the need to speak unless one is adding value to the communication process.

Show interest: Use of non-verbal cues can be utilized to signal to the one speaking that one is interested in what another is saying. The advantage that non-verbal cues have is that one does not interrupt the speaker. Examples of applicable non-verbal cues include nodding one's head, smiling and looking directly at a speaker. Appropriate non-verbal cues depend on the context within which communication is taking place. Here, one needs to be aware of the importance of culture, as some non-verbal cues have varied meanings dependent on different cultures. Looking at a speaker as an example shows interest in some cultures whilst in others, it is considered rude. While listening, one should take into consideration such challenges.

An important non-verbal cue that has an impact on whether one looks as though they have an interest in what they are saying or talking about is posture. One should ensure their posture is one that is open. This gives the message of invitation to the speaker to continue communicating. Verbal comments can also be useful as a way of showing interest. Comments to the affirmative, for example, yes or right can be used. Questions like the word really can also be utilized for the purpose of showing a speaker interest. Nonwords in the affirmative can also be used.

Summarization: As a listener, one should summarize what the speaker says. Depending on the context of the communication, this can be done internally or externally, the latter involving the speaker. For scenarios requiring to follow up, summarization is a tool that should be used to give details on the way forward in terms of what action is to be taken. Summarization also allows the listener to have a better understanding of what the speaker said, as the action makes them repeat the message to themselves. It is advisable, depending on the context within which the communication is taking place, to summarize periodically. This gives the speaker the message that the listener is still listening to them.

The Past: As a listener, one can use past conversations with a speaker to portray interest and attention. When one reminds a speaker of past conversations, the speaker feels like one that is of interest to the listener. Also, the speaker may translate the remembrance of the past by the listener as one of being important. Remembering what one said can help a listener also individualize details of a relationship with the speaker, which can help the listener stand out in the memory of the speaker.

Visualization: This involves creating a mental picture of what a speaker is communicating. It helps in cementing the message to the one listening. It also helps one stay focused on the message being communicated. One way of successfully using this tool to be a good listener is to focus one's mind on keywords being used by the speaker.

As one continues to practice the skills to improve how one listens, the more the skills will become part and parcel of who one is. As the listening skill becomes a part of one's nature, one will notice their interactions with others being more satisfactory. It should be remembered that listening is a key ingredient of communication, therefore working on becoming a good listener in turn also improves the communication skills of the listener. Listening as a skill also improves one's understanding levels. Listening is a key ingredient in negotiation skills.

Being a good listener may also end up giving one a varied perspective on issues. To become a good listener, one must have the ingredient of determination as the process of becoming one may be paved with challenges. One, though, should encourage themselves in the journey to becoming a good listener by remembering that it is a habit meaning, it is learned over time. One must consider that as with any skill to be learned, listening all begins in mind. It should be remembered that listening is the primary route through which learning does occur. There are industries like customer service that are built around the aspect of effective listening.

To be a good listener, one should focus on absorbing the information being communicated.

When one becomes an effective listener, their personality will evolve to one that is inviting. Active listening involves ensuring that the message received by the listener is accurate. Good listeners never equate hearing to active listening.

6 TIPS FOR ACTIVE LISTENING

The tips discussed in this chapter helps one develop the skill of active listening. Active listening is important in strengthening relationships and is a way through which one can offer their support to those who reach out to them. Sometimes when one is going through a rough patch, this skill can be critical in helping them not feel alone. Active listening is part and parcel of communication skills. It is preferable to remember that the process of active listening is learned over time. The tips are:

Inquire using open-ended questions: Open-ended questions are questions whose answers do not end up as yes or no. Asking open-ended questions leads to the one being asked, giving more detail in their response than a simple yes or no. This allows an individual to open up more, and get the feeling of the one asking the question wanting to know more about their point of view. It may make the one answering the questions feel relaxed and supported depending on the context within which the inquiries are being made. When asking the questions, active listening requires one to ask questions that focus on the one speaking, either in regards to the speaker as a person or the idea or emotion being communicated.

Active listening requires that one avoids changing the topic to one that moves the speaker from being the center of the communication process. The questioning tool is used in active listening for the purpose of understanding and not interrupting. The purpose stands true even if the listener feels attacked by the speaker. Not asking questions may lead to assumptions being made, which may, in turn, lead to misinterpretations that may then lead to misunderstandings. Open-ended questions encourage one to give thoughtful answers. Though using open-ended questions is an effective tool in active listening, silence, when no question of added value is available, is also powerful. Silence that is not filled by questions of no value can prompt the one being listened to, to give further clarification on the issue being communicated. One should not also focus on waiting for moments of silence in advance so as to weigh in. Doing so will inhibit effective active listening.

For one to appreciate the tool of utilizing open-ended questions in the process of active listening, one should consider the questions as to their contribution to the communication process. For organizations, the use of open-ended questions can be an effective tool that becomes a source of new ideas that they can implement to stay relevant in their industry. The information learned from this tool of active listening can be what gives an organization the competitive edge required to stay ahead of other industry players. Open-ended questioning, if used well by an active listener, can help the speaker shed light on their own flaws in mindset without them feeling as though they are being criticized.

When one uses open-ended questions effectively, it may have an effect on their ability to persuade and even increase one's social network, as one will be considered a pleasant person. The advantage of open-ended questions is that it is independent of personality type. Open-ended questioning when done right can also help organizations determine, from the customers' point of view, what they consider as the one thing they can change in order to become better, which in turn can help them move up the value chain in potential customers' minds. Open-ended questions that start with the words what and/or how, can help in breaking down resistance in the communication process, as the speaker feels that their perception of matters is of value to the active listener.

When using the open-ended questioning tool, active listening focuses on the listener being a sounding board as opposed to a solutions provider. The focus on using open-ended questions in active listening helps one avoid portraying themselves as opinionated to the speaker, a trait which is a hindrance to effective communication. As much as open-ended questions are vital tools in the skill of active listening, one must ensure that they do not ask questions over unnecessary details. Doing so is time-wasting, and a speaker may interpret the listener to be patronizing. The questioning process should focus on the main themes of the conversation.

If a speaker communicates something not understandable, it is the prerogative of the active listener to request for clarification. Ignoring the parts not understood is not advisable, as the section ignored may be a link to what the speaker will communicate later. Lack of getting clarification may, later on, portray the listener as one who is uninterested, when the speaker requests for feedback from the listener on the issue earlier raised, that the listener did not understand and did not request clarification for. Open-ended questions help one actively listen as opposed to pretending that one is listening. Open-ended questions as a tool of active listening should be used as a means of getting a greater understanding of varied issues raised by the speaker.

As powerful as the open-ended question tool is in the process of active listening if one does not learn how to use it correctly, communication will still be ineffective. Factors like the voice tone used and/or the attitude when asking questions can affect how effective the tool is in the process of communication. One should have an attitude of being open to learning and/or exploring new ideas and points of view. Also, a listener should never use open-ended questions to answer a question from the speaker. This action may be interpreted as the listener being defensive. The overall aim of using open-ended questioning as an active listening tool is to achieve the goal of mutual understanding.

Open-ended questions assist in guiding the route that a conversation takes in the context of communication. Open-ended questions are, therefore, directive in nature. Because the questions are directive in nature, they can be used to determine the focus of a conversation.

Recap*:* Recapping is a tool that is best utilized from the viewpoint of the speaker. To confirm that one has gotten the intended message of the speaker, it is useful to summarize what one feels the speaker wants to communicate. This way, miscommunication is minimized as the one speaking gets a chance to hear the message received from the point of view of the one listening. In case any clarifications are required, it can be done on the spot. Recapping also communicates to the speaker that they were being listened to. It also can give them the feeling of being understood. On the listener's side, it can improve their ability to concentrate. When recapping, it is important to focus on the big picture of what the speaker is communicating.

If one instead chooses to focus on details, the recapping tool can become a barrier to the communication process. The rule of thumb, dependent on context, is that a recap should be shorter than the speaker's communication to the listener. In an official setting, the focus should be on the overall idea while in a social setting, attention should be on the overall emotion being communicated. Recapping is best done via rephrasing. Rephrasing does not mean repeating word for word communication by the speaker but using the listener's own words, which can include keywords used by the speaker, to describe the message they are getting from the communication being transmitted by the speaker.

Recapping, as part of the tools for active listening, should never be patronizing. One way in which a listener may appear as patronizing is by overusing the recapping tool in the process of active listening. To be an effective active listener, one should recap intermittently as a way of ensuring that one has not at any time lost track of the message being transmitted by the speaker. Recapping as an essential tool to achieve active listening is best utilized after exploring the tool of using open-ended questions. Recapping is all about sharing the listener's analysis of the communication passed by the speaker.

Reflect*:* When recapping, be sure to use a part of the words or a word the speaker utilized while they spoke. This allows the speaker an opportunity to reflect on what they said and may cause them to expound more on their intended message. This technique allows the speaker to open up. Also, one should be careful not to forget what the speaker said, as when recapping the speaker may pick up that active listening was actually not taking place and stop communicating. Forgetting what a speaker said portrays the listener as one who is not really interested in what the speaker has to say.

A way through which one can brush up on the skill of recapping is by watching interviews and picking up on how this is done practically and effectively. The aim of reflection in the context of active listening is to demonstrate to the speaker that the listener has understood the message that the speaker has communicated to the listener.

Make clear: This technique can be used when the one listening is looking for clarification on a point raised by the speaker. This ensures that glossing over is avoided. As the speaker clarifies, they get a second opportunity to hear their own message repeated, which can give them better insight on the issue they are faced with.

Encourage: When listening actively, it is important not to appear to be critical towards the speaker. Though it is good to encourage, one needs to avoid filling silent periods with words. The moments of silence are important in assisting the one speaking to think through what they are feeling. It also allows the speaker to think through their next words. An active listener can encourage the speaker via non-verbal cues. Some of the non-verbal cues that can be used to encourage a speaker include facial expressions and gestures. Facial expressions, in the context of active listening, can be considered as a reflection of one's thoughts and feelings. One should, therefore, be keen on what kind of message they are portraying through their facial expressions. An example of facial expressions plus gestures that signify encouragement is a smile combined with eye contact. A way for the listener to try and ensure that the non-verbal cues they are using are suitable for the context within which the communication is taking place is to mirror the kind of gestures and expressions that the speaker is using.

To be an active listener, one should be able to encourage the speaker even if communication is being done when they are in varied locations, for example, if they are having a phone conversation. A skilled active listener is able to use this tool to save time that would be spent trying to get information through other means. While encouraging a speaker during active listening, it is crucial that one shuts down one's own mental dialogue as this may become a distraction to the goal of effective communication. One should not also fidget as it communicates distraction. To be able to use the tool of encouragement in active listening well, one must first decide mentally that they are there to listen.

Direct prompts can be used to encourage a speaker, taking into consideration the context within which the communication occurs. When using verbal cues to encourage a speaker, the listener should take care not to over encourage, which can end up distracting the speaker. If the frequency of the verbal cues is too high, one might cause the speaker to become irritated as it may seem like a means of patronizing the speaker. To manage the frequency, the listener may instead opt to give reasons for their agreement with the speaker, whilst taking care not to take the focus of the conversation away from the speaker.

In regards to using the tool of encouragement in the context of active listening, one should not give up on the active listening process early on. Sometimes, being persistent pays in getting to effective communication. Knowing though when to let go of the process is also important. Being persistent can be interpreted by the speaker that the listener is really interested in their point of view and can be a means of building trust between dialogue partners. The persistence may give the speaker the feeling of being accepted without judgment and as of value enough to be worth fighting for.

Encouragement as a tool of active listening may work well when communicating with someone over topics that one may find difficult to share, or when dealing with one exhibiting a shy personality.

Respond: Though it may seem useful not to show any kind of emotion when listening, it may appear to the speaker as disinterest. A blank expression, on the other hand, may communicate to the speaker a message of being criticized. Responding to the speaker shows them that they are acknowledged and cared for. Exhibiting a reaction can also communicate to the speaker that they are understood. It is important for a listener to give feedback to the one speaking. The feedback here should preferably be positive in nature. The feedback can either be verbal or non-verbal. In regards to verbal feedback, active listening demands that such feedback is characterized by minimal words spoken. The words are meant for encouragement, not interruption.

A reason why an active listener aims to avoid interrupting is that if they practice patience, they may find out that whatever they wanted to say, or the point of view they wanted to share, is later brought up by the speaker. Also, not interrupting as a way of utilizing the tool of response in active listening can portray the listener as one who is open to new ideas. This portrayal can be critical in solving issues, particularly when communication is occurring within the context of conflict. Interrupting a speaker while they communicate, depending on the context within which this takes place, and/or the words used, can portray the listener as one who is abrasive. The listener may also lose the respect that the speaker has towards them as the speaker may interpret the interruption as a sign of immaturity. This perception by the speaker can lead to a communication breakdown. It is important while responding, particularly in the work context, to let the speaker know, if applicable, what will be done as a follow up to the communication. In social contexts, follow up can be in the form of going back to the topic discussed previously, with the individual in question the next time one comes across them. Follow up can also be done via email, through social media, or even via a text message.

It is important that if from communicating with the one speaking, one feels that the speaker is in imminent danger, for example, one considering committing suicide, that one seeks for help urgently. In such scenarios, it is crucial that the listener stays in contact and even accompanies the speaker to the point where they are to be assisted. Active listeners are aware of the power of posture in terms of what message it gives to the speaker and how it can be used to signify response. To appear approachable, an active listener should choose an open posture. To show that one is actively listening, one may choose the posture of leaning forward. Having the right posture assists an active listener, to give signals to their brain that they should be focusing on the speaker. A posture that exhibits listening is when the listener directs their body towards the speaker—doing the opposite exhibits disinterest or lack of attentive listening.

Placing the head on the hand can also be interpreted by the speaker as one is actively listening to them. It is said that a larger percentage of communication is non-verbal in nature. Active listening requires that the listener indicates through cues, attention to the speaker, depending on the context. Active listening requires that one is fully focused on the process of listening. To avoid getting distracted, particularly by mental criticisms, an active listener should endeavor to focus on the message being transmitted as opposed to the speaker. It should be noted that mental criticisms come from the clash of one's beliefs and values and the ideas that one feels the speaker is trying to push. Any urge to carry out other activities in tandem with listening should be shunned. Multi-tasking and active listening are incompatible.

Part of the cues active listening utilizes includes nodding, smiling, eye contact, and facing a speaker. One should note though that smiling can portray to the speaker agreement, and should, therefore, be used only if one is in agreement to the message being communicated by the speaker or is happy with it. When combined with nodding, it signifies understanding and listening. Smiles plus eye contact can denote encouragement. In regards to eye contact, the goal for the listener should be at all times to maintain contact that is comfortable for both the listener and the speaker, by taking into consideration the context within which the communication is taking place. To be an effective active listener, one should use cues that are suitable to a situation. What may make sense in one situation may not be appropriate for another. Active listeners can read cues even when a speaker is not physically present. They can do so via listening, e.g., to the voice tone over a phone conversation. Although active listening requires a response, it is important not to interrupt the speaker. Interrupting a speaker can be viewed as an attempt at multi-tasking, which curtails effective communication. One will through interruption not get the full message as intended by the speaker. One should wait for an appropriate time to respond, e.g., when the speaker pauses or when they are looking for a response from the listener.

In this age of technology, remember that interruptions can be due to gadgets that we frequently use, like phones ringing or checking emails.

Responding may also mean requesting for postponement of when the communication can take place, to a time when one can actively listen. Being responsive may also mean that the active listener chooses an environment for the communication to take place, which is conducive for effective listening. In regards to active listening, one should not confuse responding and reacting. Being responsive also means an active listener ensures that they are able to hear what the speaker is saying. If they are unable to, they can raise the concern, or adjust the volume, actions dependent on the context of the communication process. Requesting for clarification in such a context is part of being a responsive active listener.

Being responsive should involve being patient as well. To use the tool of response effectively in active listening, one should consider the process of listening as an opportunity to learn and grow. Response as a tool in active listening should not involve giving advice or solutions to the speaker. Instead, the focus should be on assisting the speaker in getting their own solutions. One should not give in to the urge of sharing a comparison on how they handled a similar issue. In regards to response, active listening requires that one incorporates mirroring. This is when one subtly mirrors the non-verbal cues of the speaker. This creates a subconscious bond between the speaker and the active listener.

Response from an active listener's perspective is always empathetic. When responding during active listening, one should take care not to make the speaker feel rushed, as this may lead to the speaker holding back, leading to ineffective communication. When responding, one should aim to match the levels of energy that the speaker demonstrates in their communication. Doing so allows the listener to be in sync emotionally with the speaker. Demonstration of similar energy levels will also save time as the speaker might not feel the need to repeat the message. Examples that demonstrate energy levels include exhibiting excitement when a speaker shares the good news. When responding, it is important in active listening to respond at the understanding level of the speaker. Doing so helps one not to appear as patronizing to the speaker and for the speaker to feel that they have been understood.

A way within which a listener can demonstrate a response to the speaker, dependent on the context within which the communication process occurs, is to take notes. As much as one may have the urge to plan for a response to the speaker, while they are still speaking, it is best to plan the response after they finish speaking. One should not give in to the thought that they do not want to be caught unawares. This is because unless the speaker finishes communicating, e.g., a point, the listener makes the presumption that they have said all that is to be said, and might find themselves totally off what the speaker intended to communicate.

Being responsive may also mean being aware that the speaker is not in a mindset of wanting to speak, and having the skill to let go of the conversation until a suitable time. One should also be able to tell via the cues the speaker gives when the speaker has completed communicating. It is also important to note that not all communication from the speaker requires a response. A listener should also be aware that just because they respond, does not automatically mean that the speaker will choose to align themselves with the viewpoint of the listener. The listener should take care not to get offended in case their ideas or solutions are rejected, but instead should consider the response as part of the communication process.

The speaker might consider the responses from the listeners as inappropriate for the situation they are facing. The listener should be aware too that there are times that no matter how well one uses the response tool, in the context of active listening, no solution is arrived at, and that the solution may be arrived at later by the speaker away from the context of the current conversation they are having. If such a scenario unfolds, the listener should take respite, in the possibility that the active listening process initiated by the listener, had some positive contribution to the solution later arrived at.

Also in regards to the response tool, the listener must remember that they have no right to demand that the speaker shares with them the solution that they have arrived at, during or from the active listening process. When an active listener responds, they should do so in a relaxed manner so as not to portray oneself in an awkward way that may make the speaker uncomfortable, which may lead to ineffective communication. When responding, an active listener may use visualization as a means of maintaining attention on the speaker. To be effective in active listening, one should take note of words or phrases used repeatedly by the speaker as these may give an indication of the underlying emotions that they are dealing with or feeling.

A way through which an active listener can respond well to the speaker is by training themselves to slow down one's level of mental thought processes to the speed of the speaker's rate of communication. Doing so can help dull the urge to interrupt the speaker. Any time one gets the urge to respond at the inappropriate time, one should take it as a signal that one is not actively listening. For active listening to be effective, particularly in the context of utilizing the response tool, one should aim to expand their knowledge in varied topics, so as to be able to respond meaningfully if need be. Being knowledgeable in a topic a speaker is discussing may also help an active listener respond patiently. Understanding the context within which communication is occurring will help an active listener respond appropriately.

One should always try not to get involved in active listening when they are overworked and/or stressed as they might not be in the best position mentally, to be effective at responding actively. Also, when one does not respond effectively, they are in essence wasting time, a resource that can never be regained. An effective response by an active listener may make the speaker get a feeling of being supported. Response as a tool of active listening requires that the listener is honest. This can be exemplified by asking for clarification in case a listener is distracted and misses the point raised by the speaker.

For the response tool to assist in active listening, the listener even when faced with difficult conversations, should aim to respond in a way that leads to a win-win outcome of the conversation. An active listener should avoid responding through justification as this tends to inhibit the speaker from coming up with their own solutions. To utilize the tool of response effectively in active listening, one should remember that a speaker having a varied view of an issue from one's own, does not necessarily mean their view is wrong; it may simply mean there are varied viewpoints towards an issue.

To be an effective active listener, one should before responding, find out whether the speaker is looking for an opportunity to be heard or if they are looking for solutions. Finding this out gives an indication on the direction in which the responding tool of active listening should be used. Whilst using the response tool of active listening, if one has to choose between listening to words and/or emotions, it is best to choose the latter, as understanding the latter will lead one to understand the words in most cases. The advantage that responding effectively has as a tool of active listening is that the listener has an opportunity to change how they are to respond as the speakers continue conversing, based on new information they may get from the speaker over time.

When focusing on developing listening skills, remember that more talking does not necessarily equate to better communication. It can actually be a barrier to being an effective communicator. The golden rule here is to aim to listen more than talk. Aiming to become an active listener makes one effective at communication. The skill of active listening is considered an important part of being an effective leader. For some industries like sales and customer care, active listening skills can mean the difference between success and failure. To effectively use the tips discussed to become an active listener, one must have a high sense of self-awareness.

Being self-aware allows one to have an honest outlook of where they are on the journey of becoming an active listener. It helps in taking note of the challenges one faces on this journey. Being able to do this helps one know where to work on to improve their skill of active listening. For organizations, incorporating these tips can be an aid in hiring the right team member. The advantage of the tips is that they work dually. As one practices active listening, one will probably be also listened to better. Active listening stands on the foundation of putting others before oneself. It is a skill that requires sacrifice.

In regards to active listening, the listener should never forget the speaker's name. Forgetting the name of the speaker may portray to the speaker that the listener is disrespectful or does not find them to be of value. The key to active listening being effective is that one should be self-aware enough to know if they are in the right mindset to put someone else's communication needs ahead of their own. Just as it is important to know when one has the right mindset for active listening, one should also be able to tell when they not in the right mindset to be an effective active listener.

To improve one's ability to listen actively, one may make the decision to practice this skill within their immediate social network. Doing so may give the active listener an opportunity to get feedback on how their skill level is improving or not. In order not to give up on the process of learning the skill of active listening, one must remember that the initial stages of practicing this skill might feel out of place, as though one is not authentic. One should continue pushing their limits until the skill becomes part and parcel of who they are. In order not to feel awkward, one should remember that though it may feel inauthentic to the active listener, the speaker, on the other hand, maybe none the wiser to the thought process of the one practicing the active listening skills.

For one to be an effective active listener, one must always remember to use context as the overall factor that determines which tool is appropriate for the varied communication processes that they may be involved in.

IMPROVE YOUR LISTENING SKILLS WITH ACTIVE LISTENING

One way of improving listening skills is to look at listening as an opportunity to gather information from various sources and even learn something new in some cases. One should also be able to retain what was communicated, whose percentage can indicate how well one is, at becoming an active listener. One should consider the improvement of listening skills via active listening as a means of self-development.

One should look at communication as a two-way street. To be a better listener, one must train their minds not to wander off to other topics off what a speaker is communicating. One should also not focus on how they are going to respond to what is being communicated as this takes their mind away from focusing on listening, to the future of how they are going to respond. It should be remembered that active listening involves making a conscious choice to listen with the aim of getting the full message being communicated.

Those in leadership positions would do well to work on improving their listening skills, as they are prone to be distracted by the varied tasks expected of them at any one time. Improving one's listening skills as a leader will help one stem from the feeling of isolation that sometimes is described as part and parcel of being in management. Active listening can also assist those in leadership positions to solve problems that may arise in varied scenarios they come across.

Active listening can be achieved in a myriad of ways, including:

Paying attention: As obvious as this may sound, paying attention is critical in improving the skill of active listening. For the tool of paying attention to be effective in active listening, the active listener should prepare their mindset in advance. Preparing can mean reading around a topic so that one has a better chance at understanding the subject of the communication e.g., vocabulary that is used within certain industries. Doing so assists an active listener to follow the main themes of the subject matter easily than instead spending time trying to understand what certain words that the speaker is using mean. Moreover, the preparation will also help bring the understanding level of the active listener closer or equal to the speaker making effective communication easier to achieve. Also, one should understand the difference between listening and hearing, with the latter being defined as one's capability to perceive sound.

This tool of improving listening skills requires that it is done with a purpose. The purposes can be varied for e.g., helping one stem the negative habit of procrastination, by willing oneself to pay attention to issues as they occur in the context of active listening. Also paying attention can be a way through which an opportunity is provided to a speaker.

Attention can be achieved, for example, by looking at the person speaking. Here, one should take into consideration the implication of doing so within cultural contexts as some cultures would consider looking at someone directly as a sign of rudeness. When appropriate, one should face the speaker as a means of improving their active listening skills.

One should try and ignore distractions that may occur in their environment so as to fully focus on the speaker. Also, one should focus on the themes raised by the speaker as over-analyzing details of the message, may end up becoming a source of distraction. The ability to pick up main themes in a communication process can be referred to as filtering. A skilled active listener is able to filter by first understanding the reason behind the subject of the communication as it generally gives a reflection of what is important in the conversation. The reason behind the subject of the communication process occurring can be looked at from either the viewpoint of the active listener or of that of their conversation partner. The overall themes thus filtered are the lens through which an active, effective listener approaches all parts of the communication. Approaching communication this way keeps in mind at all times the context within which the communication is taking place, which is important as it determines the perception portrayed of the message being communicated. Once the filtering process is done, synthesizing the information by the active speaker comes into play. The process of synthesizing will then automatically lead an active listener to visualization. One should do all within their power to get rid of distractions that either occur internally or externally. Part of getting rid of internal distractions is the ability to be self-aware. In the context of active listening, self-awareness is about being cognizant of one's feelings and emotions and the reason behind them. Also, an active listener should go through a process of self-analysis to find out what usually is a source of distraction for them, then work on those things no longer being a distraction to the communication process they are involved in at any one time. So, for example, if one notices that it is usually phone calls that act as a distraction in the context within which they are in, they can choose to put their phone on silent mode or if it calls for it, even switch it off just for the process of effective communication to take place through active listening. Internal distractions can also sometimes be referred to as a psychological type of distraction or noise. Internal distractions can involve focusing on the gender the speaker belongs to, their race or even the color of their skin. One may even find themselves biased against or towards someone based on what they do for a living. Focusing on such distractions add no value to the communication process in most cases. The mannerisms of a speaker can also become a distraction to the process of effective active listening if one chooses to focus on them instead of focusing on the value of the message being communicated. Such distractions generally affect the process of effective communication by making the listener view the speaker through an emotionally driven lens. It can be also about, if possible, having communication in an environment that is conducive to both parties.

The attention portrayed in active listening should be one that exhibits empathy, which is the act of mentally putting oneself in another person's situation. Doing this can help in building an emotional connection between the listener and the speaker.

Paying attention can be done both verbally and non-verbally, with the latter including the use of body language. One should remember that body language has the power to determine the level of focus one can give to a speaker.

To keep one's attention on the speaker, one can aim to maintain breathing slowly and deeply. The breathing technique can also help the speaker stay calm, particularly if the context of the communication may lead to the buildup of an apprehensive environment.

Visualization is a tool that one can use to pay attention when actively listening.

One should also endeavor to main neutral mentally as the opposite will lead one to become critical, which in turn will lessen their attention level towards the speaker. An active listener should be careful not to be critical even of the non-verbal cues that they perceive as being exhibited by the speaker, as this can also lead to a breakdown of ineffective communication. The focus of the active listener in such a scenario is to recognize its existence or occurrence.

To improve one's listening skills with active listening in the context of paying attention, one can incorporate the tool of mirroring, which involves subtly exhibiting the same non-verbal cues like the one portrayed by the speaker—at a subconscious level, mirroring acts to cement the bond between the speaker and the listener, as the speaker will not feel judged. One, though, must be careful not to exhibit mirroring that is not in tandem with their point of view on what the speaker is saying.

The key with non-verbal cues in the context of paying attention is to aim to strike the right balance between being comfortable and showcasing interest. The active listener should not put their feelings even of anxiety at the forefront as it may change the environment within which the communication is taking place in a negative manner. One way that an active listener can prevent focusing on their own negative emotions is by changing their mindset to one that knows that their role in the communication process is not one of performance. Changing one's thought processes in this manner diminishes the aspect of feeling like one needs to fulfill expectations.

If one is looking to move the speaker from one point to the next, one can use the tool of summarization for such an action.

To improve one's listening skills, one should also take the mindset of being sacrificial. This means that the listener should not view the activity of active listening as one that makes them less than the one they are listening to. It may seem awkward depending on the social dynamics, yet it is an important mindset shift that needs to happen if at all, one is truly determined to hone their skillset as regards active listening. A true active listener comes from the point of humility.

For a listener to be an effective active listener, one should consider creating an environment that is conducive for the communication to take place. The preparations to be done in this context are both physical and mental in nature. The preparations for effective communication to take place should be done in advance, if possible. The preparation could involve having a list of inquiries that one needs more information on. The advance preparation can help an active listener continually keep their focus on the speaker.

To be an effective active listener, one may have to ask the speaker to slow down the rate at which they are communicating, dependent on the media through which the conversation is taking place. This is to ensure that they are able to keep pace with the speaker and the message they are transmitting. If communication is e.g., occurring via digital media, one can choose to slow down the speed at which it is at.

Time is a factor that should be considered in terms of its effect on the ability of one to actively listen. Communications should last for periods that are not so long that one struggles to keep their focus on the speaker, but instead should be tailored according to the individual optimal spans of attention as regards the one's communication. For e.g., children have a shorter attention span in comparison to adults and may find it difficult to pay attention continuously over long periods of time. In some cases, if a speaker also converses for too long, they may lose the trail of the initial topic of interest.

A skilled active listener is able to use the tool of paying attention to give encouragement to the speaker, which in turn leads to an increase in the communication quality.

Use cues: Non-verbal cues and verbal cues can be used to achieve active listening. The cues signal to the speaker that they have one's full attention. Active listeners who are skilled are able to understand the cues being exhibited by the speaker, know what is of importance to the speaker. Non-verbal cues are sometimes referred to as subtexts. Reading the non-verbal cues exhibited by the speaker also allows one to tell if they are connecting with the speaker, or if they need to continue working on the connection. Non-verbal cues that can be used to improve listening skills in the context of active listening include nodding, which may signify understanding of the message on the part of the listener, and/or agreement, depending on the context within which the communication is taking place. A smile may also have the same effect as a nod with the additional significance of exhibiting happiness. A nod can also signify that a listener is actively mentally processing the information that is being shared by the speaker. The smile is a non-verbal cue that can be suitable when communication is occurring in a tense context, as it may assist in diffusing tension. A smile can signify, depending on the context that a listener is not on the defensive. The non-verbal cue of eye contact can, depending on the context, signify encouragement. Maintaining eye contact, apart from portraying a listener in a positive way, dependent on the context within which active listening is taking place, can be a way in which one is able to listen attentively. Leaning forward as an example of a non-verbal cue can signify attention on the speaker who can also be signified via pointing or directing one's body towards that of the speaker, dependent on the context within which the communication is taking place. Posture is another non-verbal cue that is of importance in the process of active listening. Eye movements are classified as non-verbal cues, and skilled listeners can be able to tell the emotions of a speaker by watching their eyes. Other non-verbal cues that active listeners can look out for are the volume and pitch of the speaker's voice as changes in these may change the meaning of the message they intend to communicate. Non-verbal cues can be noted through both watching and listening to the speaker. To improve one's listening skill, one should always note when verbal and non-verbal clues clash, as this may be an indication that the speaker is emotional. Non-verbal cues can give an active listener a glimpse of the personality traits of a speaker.

The cultural and context effect that affects cues should always be taken into consideration in order to improve active listening skills. This is because these two factors can completely change the meaning and appropriateness of the use of cues at any given time.

One should note that cues work both ways in that it portrays an underlying message from both the speaker's and listener's point of view. To improve on one's listening skills with active listening, one should endeavor to understand the meaning of varied cues that occur within a communication process, taking into account how context affects the interpretation of these cues.

For one to be able to understand cues as a way to improve listening skills, one should continuously practice the same. Cues can also be a way through which an active listener is able to showcase to the speaker that they are able to process the information that the speaker is sharing.

Understanding cues and their meanings within context is critical in, e.g., dissolving conflicts.

Cues are a subtle way of participating in communication without the negative effect of interruption.

Cues should come from a place of empathy, as doing so can be a way through which an active listener gets to be trusted by a speaker.

When utilizing cues as a means of being effective in active listening, a listener should endeavor not to portray oneself as defensive, as doing so may frustrate the speaker or exhibit to them the listener's lack of cooperation.

Verbal cues as a tool in active listening, become more crucial when those communicating are unable to see each other, e.g., in scenarios whereby communication is via email and/or phone calls. Though non-verbal cues have their place, overusing them, like, through continuous repetition of the same words can cause them to become a source of distraction and interruption, which an active listener would want to avoid. The speaker may also perceive the continuous repetitive verbal response as a sign that the listener is disinterested in the conversation, which may lead to a breakdown of effective communication.

Feedback: When one responds to what a speaker is communicating, it enhances the active listening process. The response to the speaker should always be made from the point of respect, even if the response is one that does not agree with the point of view of the speaker.

Feedback can assist in the request for clarification on areas that the listener did not clearly understand. Clarification received in this manner can allow the listener to understand the mindset of the speaker. It can also be utilized when the listener is looking for further discussions on the topic that the speaker is presenting.

Using paraphrasing when giving feedback, gives an opportunity for both the speaker and the listener to confirm that they are on the same page, in regards to the message being communicated. It allows the listener's understanding of the speaker's message to be solidified. Paraphrasing allows for both parties to be able to reflect on what is being communicated. Paraphrasing can be looked at as a form of mirroring. This tool allows one to get rid of misconceptions that are sometimes clouded by pre-conceived notions. It is also a tool that the one who is actively listening can use to exhibit their understanding of the subject matter that is being shared by the speaker. Paraphrasing, though should not be presumed to be an indication of agreement. Paraphrasing can also showcase the active listener to the speaker as one who is caring.

One can also use questions to provide feedback during active listening. To encourage probing and therefore, a more detailed response, one should utilize the power of open-ended questions. Other kinds of questions that can be utilized in the context of active listening include leading questions and even closed-ended questions, depending on the goal of the communication process at any one time. The foundation of the questions used as a means of engaging in feedback as one works on their listening skills is that the questions should be specific in nature. The feedback tool of active listening should be utilized by active listeners, if possible, to challenge every assumption that they notice they came with into the communication process. This can be done via the feedback tool of questioning. Remember that the tool of questioning can be used by the active listener to feed their curiosity on various aspects of the communication being received from the speaker. One should consider the active listening tool of questioning as a means through which the active listener can get answers to any inquiries they might have on the subject of interest to the speaker. In almost every communication scenario, it is important to ask at least one question as not doing so may portray the listener to the speaker as one who is not truly listening. In regards to the questioning tool of active listening, the active listener should only use it after they have listened to the speaker communicating and never before the communication has begun.

The correct kind of feedback should portray the goal of offering support to the speaker. The speaker should feel that the active listener is welcoming of their communication. One should remember that the goal of feedback is not necessarily about being in agreement but of showcasing respect to the speaker. One should aim via active listening, using the tool of feedback, to build trust and rapport with the speaker. If this tool is used correctly, one can be able to validate the speaker. Whenever one is providing feedback, one should aim to enhance a positive environment. A way through a positive environment can be achieved in order to aid the tool of feedback as part of developing the skills of active listening is the removal of physical barriers, e.g., tables between the speaker and the listener, depending on the context within which the communication is taking place. Removal of the barriers portrays an environment that is safe and trustworthy. The purpose of feedback should be to find new ways to connect with the speaker and/or their message. An advantage of feedback as a tool of active listening is that it can help one keep their attention on the speaker if at all, they feel that their attention is wavering. If one finds that the speaker is getting off-topic, they can use questions in the context of feedback to get the speaker back to their original topic. This skill is particularly useful in work environments where people prefer having meetings that are short and purposeful. The feedback that directs the conversation back to the speaker can be referred to as supportive feedback whilst the ones that take the conversation can be referred to as shift type of feedback. Shift feedback can be considered to be narcissistic in nature. An active listener should not use the tool of feedback within the active listening context to defend their personal views. The only scenario where one is allowed to shift part of the focus away from the speaker is when one shares a point that is of mutual benefit to both the speaker and the active listener. Sharing in this manner can help an active listener portray empathy towards the speaker.

Those who learn how to improve their listening skills via active listening end up growing in their skill levels, which in a business setting can translate to business growth. Feedback is also a means through which active listening can help one learn something new.

At first, practicing the process of feedback may feel unnatural, and leave one feeling awkward, but as one keeps working on improving the skill of active listening, using feedback as a tool of active listening will become part of one's nature.

To improve active listening, one should aim to give feedback that is empathetic. To practice empathetic, active listening, one must be able to exercise patience. Sharing empathetic feedback gives the speaker a feeling of being heard. Using the power of empathy when sharing feedback also helps in gauging what kind of response is suitable in the context within which the communication is occurring, as one will be in tune with the emotions of the speaker. It should be noted that an empathetic, active listener facilitates effective communication.

It should be noted that body language is also a means through which feedback can be exhibited. One, though, should ensure that the body language they choose to use, does not end up being a form of distraction. One should take note that sometimes distractions can lead to the speaker ending up being frustrated or uncomfortable, which may, in turn, curtail the process of improving the skills of active listening. One should be aware that the act of being still is sometimes enough to portray a positive body language. Depending on the context within which the feedback is occurring, it may showcase focus on the part of the one who is actively listening.

Feedback should be given in a summarized manner with the aim being for the feedback to be shorter than the message passed by the speaker, whilst taking into consideration the context within which the feedback occurs. One can use notes to be able to summarize effectively, and as a means of keeping track of the feedback they intend to share when it is appropriate to do so. Depending on the context within which the notes are taken, the one being listened to may consider it as a sign of respect.

One should remember that feedback as a tool of improving active listening is not about solving problems, but instead a pathway through which the speaker can be directed to get a solution to the challenges they are facing.

Feedback may also involve, depending on the context within which the communication is taking place, sharing with the speaker the intended way forward.

For one to be efficient at actively listening, one should make peace with the standard of formulating responses during the appropriate pauses or breaks from the speaker. Interrupting the speaker at inappropriate times may lead them to lose respect for the listener, and dependent on the context of the communication, it may lead to a loss of an opportunity, even for effective communication. As much as it is important to share feedback in the process of communication, one should also be comfortable with silences. One should not let their emotions, even supposedly a positive one like enthusiasm take over the need to accept silence as an effective tool of active listening.

In the context of feedback, to improve listening skills, one should use simple language in communicating. If one chooses language that is complex or one that the other person cannot understand, e.g., due to a barrier in language, they introduce a form of distraction in the communication process, sometimes referred to as semantic distractions, which will, in turn, curtail the effectiveness of communication. The best bet is to use the same level of complexity in language as the speaker. This way, the listener does not end up portraying themselves as being patronizing. To be an effective listener, one should also focus on the type of language used. It is best to mirror the language used being sensitive to cultural contexts and meanings of words used. The use of complex language during feedback can cause the active listener to portray oneself as a show-off, which may, in turn, negate the communication process. The feedback from the active listener should be one that the speaker is able to understand and preferably be able to relate to easily. When an active listener responds in a way that the speaker is able to relate to, a rapport may be created between the speaker and the active listener, which will, in turn, enhance communication.

One should also be self-aware of their voice tone in a bid to improve their listening skills through active listening. It is important that the voice tone used can change the intended meaning of the feedback being shared. Also, one should match the voice tone being used to the situation within which the conversation is taking place.

Effective use of feedback to improve one's listening skills in the context of active listening requires that one has a high state of emotional intelligence. The ability to be emotionally intelligent can help one to improve their active listening skills as one can be able to manage both their emotions and that of the speaker, ensuring that the process of communication is not affected negatively.

An effective active listener should also be able to use feedback as a way of accepting criticism towards them that is constructive in nature. When it is the listener who is giving the criticism, it should be constructive in nature and balanced.

To improve active listening skills with active listening, one should not allow details like the speaker's accent to become a distraction from their focus on the message being transmitted.

In terms of the environment required for feedback, one should match the type of feedback with an environment suitable for the same. For e.g., important information can be given in environments void of any distractions. Distractions inhibit the free flow of communication that makes active listening effective.

Avoid interruptions: Depending on the context within which communication is occurring, it is important to avoid interrupting the speaker. One should wait until the speaker is finished or gives the go-ahead for the listener to respond, for them to chime in. To succeed at active listening, one should discourage interruptions even from other people who are not the speaker.

Interruptions can sometimes be viewed as a sign of lack of interest, disrespect and even of one being rude. If at all one has to interrupt, it is prudent to let the speaker finish their point fast. If one feels that the speaker has stayed in monologue for an extended period of time, depending on the context of the communication process, one may at an appropriate time e.g. during a pause, use questions which are closed – ended to lead the speaker towards completion of their message.

When one interrupts, there is an increase in the possibility of the arising of misunderstandings and missing parts of the message that the speaker intended to communicate.

The advantage of developing the skill of active listening is that one is able to receive much more information than when not listening actively. Career-wise, this skill can determine how fast one moves up the corporate ladder. For example, for those with sales roles, the skill is critical in carrying out their work. It helps in building relationships with clients that are successful. Even within the family and personal relationship setting, active listening is a critical skill. Socially, one can expand the number of friendships by working on this skill. When people feel listened to and hopefully understood, they are more likely to bond faster.

To be an effective active listener, one should take into account both the emotional and intellectual portions of communication. The emotional portion, whether positive or negative, can lead to the breakdown of effective active listening and communication.

It is important to note that anyone who continuously chooses to work on their listening skills with active listening will notice an improvement over time.

HOW TO MAKE SOMEONE REMEMBER YOU FOR A LIFETIME

There are individuals who have mastered the art of communication so much so that strangers open up to them about their vulnerabilities. Such people stick on to memories for lengths of time. They are said to have the ability to have a presence that is defined as being captivating. There are those who have mastered the skill of active listening and are using it to generate wealth. This is exemplified in the lives of those who host talk shows. Active listening allows one to become a connector. It allows individuals to easily and naturally connect with others even if contact with the other is over a short period of time. It allows the connection to occur even if it is the first time that the dialogue partners are meeting. The tools shared in this chapter can be used in various settings, including professional and social ones. There are tools that one can use in order to form a connection with others, including:

Stage setting: This involves creating an environment e.g., through word or speech that makes the one being communicated with feel relaxed and at ease. It can also be done literally by setting the place of meeting to be in a location within which one would feel relaxed. Also, one can reach out to the other person by going to where they are or coming close to them. This setting allows for intimate conversations to occur.

Simple strategies like ensuring there are no physical barriers between those communicating goes a long way in setting the stage. Physical barriers can include things like desks or tables. Removing these makes the environment seem more intimate and less intimidating.

Even in social settings, setting the stage makes a difference. One can choose to sit adjacent to the one they are wanting to make a connection with as opposed to across them, of course, taking into consideration the cultural context of the same.

Non-verbal cues do play a role in a stage setting with the crossing of hands, sending the message of one not ready to be intimate or vulnerable. When one is open, one tends to connect socially and even physically, the latter, occurring via the sense of touch which can be achieved through hugs. When it comes to touch, it is important to think of whether the person on the receiving end will find it offensive or welcoming.

The focus should be on what can be termed as platonic touches. Such touches lead to the connection as opposed to creating offense. Platonic touches have the ability to lower barriers to communication.

A way that one can also set the stage to be memorable is for one to remember the name of one's dialogue partner and depending on the context, if appropriate, use it to address them. Remembering one's name is, in essence, acknowledging them, which can make one memorable. Also, for one to stick out in someone's memory, one should never forget to share out their names with those they have conversations with. To make it even easier for others to remember, one can choose to relate their names to something that is easy to remember. Their names can represent something that would make their audience have a higher ability to create a mental memory in one's dialogue partner. For those who have names that may pose difficulty in remembering, one may choose to break it down for their dialogue partner or shorten it to a level that makes it easy for one to remember.

Stage setting can also be done by presenting an individual with a gift that is of something of value to them. This way, every time they see the gift or better yet, use it, they will remember the one who gave them the gift. One should remember that the gift does not have to be expensive. The focus instead should be how relevant the gift is to the intended receiver of the gift.

Stage setting can also be achieved by one being uniquely them e.g., in the way one dresses. When one stands out from the crowd, the possibility of being forgotten lessens considerably. Also, when one is authentically themselves, they tend to have a positive effect on others in that they become comfortable in also being who they truly are. What this does is that it, in turn, leads to a relaxed atmosphere that makes one memorable. The reason why authenticity works is that the memory here involves both dialogue partners, and in a positive light.

Using the power of intrigue is also a means through which stage setting can be achieved as a tool of being memorable. This can be done via sharing just enough information to hold the attention of a dialogue partner as they wait expectantly for the rest of the details. Intrigue is created by how information is shared. To achieve the right balance, one should give enough information to pique one's interest and yet not answer all the inquiries they have concerning the subject being communicated. In this context, questions are answered in a way that creates more interest to have more inquiries. To create intrigue, one must have the ability to know what kind of information to give and over what time period. To create intrigue, one must create a balance between rewarding one's curiosity whilst creating more questions. Sharpening this skill allows one to know not to give too much information to one who is not interested in getting to know more. This can be looked at from the point of showing respect to one's dialogue partner in that one does not want to overwhelm their conversation partner with information that they have little to no interest in. In the context of intrigue, one should answer the questions in a way that does not portray them as being defensive, as this, in turn, can negate any interest that the dialogue partner has. When sharing information in the context of intrigue, one must always respond to inquiries authentically for one to be memorable.

Context on its own is an important part of the skill of stage setting as it can determine whether or not one remains memorable. The surrounding within which communication takes place, as an example, can make one memorable. The right context can make someone stand out from the rest of the crowd in a positive light. To use the tool of context well for the stage setting, one must be highly self-aware.

Stage setting can also be achieved via the use of a setting that is void of distractions when in conversation with people. This can have the effect of being memorable as one's dialogue partner is in a context that encourages full attention.

In regard to stage setting as a means to remain memorable in others' minds, one must be able to know when it is time to let go of a conversation. One wants to do this when the dialogue partner is still interested in the conversations. Otherwise, the conversation may drag on unnecessarily, resulting in one's dialogue partner looking to get away from them as opposed to remembering them.

One should always set the stage to be remembered by looking at interactions from a legacy point of view, i.e., how one can impact someone else's life in a positive manner. To create such an impact, the focus should be on how one can help someone else.

Follow up is a way to set the stage for one to be remembered. This can be done either in a social or professional setting. Following up on conversations with dialogue partners can cause the budding of friendly relationships in both professional and social settings, as the other parties feel that they are important. Follow up, in essence, gives the message that one is willing to sacrifice the resource that cannot be regenerated that is time for the sake of someone else. Follow up is a tool that is sacrificial in nature. For an effective follow-up, one should tailor the process appropriately, taking into consideration the context within which communication is taking place. Follow-ups can be made effective by being specific on responses tailored according to information gathered for e.g., during past conversations. Follow up, if possible, should be on a consistent basis, particularly when one is looking to grow the strength of the memory and/or relationship formed.

Taking the initiative is a great way in which to use stage setting as a tool to make one memorable to others. Taking the initiative can be in the form of reaching out to someone or being the coordinator for the meet up among friends. These actions cause one to be a connector. Connectors are remembered easily as they generally feature along with varied social networks. Depending on the activities one coordinate, particularly those that make one remember positive memories, one can be memorable. One should look at taking the initiative as a means through which they can increase the strength and size of their social network.

One should avoid going mute if they intend to set the stage for meaningful conversation as others may consider it as an indication that they do not want to be engaged in communication.

One can utilize the tool of open-ended questions as a means of getting others to hold conversations with them. These questions are those that cannot be responded to by specific answers. As one shares their viewpoints based on an inquiry from an open-ended question, they may end up being relaxed enough and remember the one who gave them an opportunity to be heard.

Eye contact: This should be looked at within the context of culture as in some scenarios, maintaining eye contact is considered rude or intimidating. For some cultures, maintaining eye contact is considered as a sign of respect, of one listening to another and even a form of intimacy. It can make the speaker feel understood. It makes the listener seem present. Maintaining appropriate levels of eye contact can also portray the listener as one who is caring. Eye contact can be used to portray confidence, which is an important ingredient of being memorable.

Non-verbal Cues: Nodding, squinting, smiling are some examples of non-verbal cues that can help in connecting with others.

Smiling as a non-verbal cue can portray confidence, which is an important ingredient in making someone memorable.

Posture is a non-verbal cue that can also be used to portray confidence when conversing with a dialogue partner. To achieve the right balance of confidence, one needs to portray a posture that is open. The right posture can be achieved e.g., via maintaining a straight posture. One should aim not to fidget as this may diminish their aura of confidence. One should also avoid the urge to slouch. A handshake that is firm, depending on the context within which communication is playing out, can be considered as a sign of being confident. One should aim for the right balance when it comes to the characteristic of being confident, as one does not want to portray themselves as being arrogant and/or stern, two traits that do not augur well with being memorable.

These cues utilized in the art of active listening help one know that what they are saying is of interest to the listener. These help one feel that the listener is genuinely interested in understanding what their viewpoints on issues are. Non-verbal cues have the ability to make individuals feel appreciated. One should be careful, therefore not to exhibit non-verbal cues that portray e.g., disinterest if they are looking to be remembered positively by their conversation partner for a long time. When one e.g., pretends to be interested in what their conversation partner has to say, the non-verbal cues, in most cases, will betray their dishonesty.

Non-verbal cues can be used as a tool that showcases an individual as being approachable, which is a factor that can determine if one will actually engage in a conversation, which in turn, depending on how the conversation goes, can lead to one being considered as memorable. One should think of non-verbal cues as a reflection that other individuals see of what is their thoughts and should, therefore, aim to align them to the message they are sending to the world.

Handshakes and hugs are non-verbal cues that can be utilized in the journey of making one memorable. The key thing here is that one should be aware of the effect of context, even cultural, on what is considered appropriate or not.

To be effective in using non-verbal cues as a tool of making one memorable, it is advisable to tailor the tool to what an individual finds comfortable. Being comfortable in this case should be looked at from the viewpoint of the one who someone is looking to interact with. The idea here is to mirror the comfort levels of one's dialogue partner when it comes to utilizing non-verbal cues.

Paraphrase: The tool of paraphrasing or recapping cannot be overstated. This allows one to ensure that they are getting the message that the speaker is intent on passing. This allows a connection as the speaker feels that the listener is intent on understanding where they are coming from, and understands why they feel the way they do. Paraphrasing works best when one comes from the point of view of sacrificial humility, which is the putting up of others' interest before one's own.

When paraphrasing, using keywords or phrases that were used by one's conversation partner in statements, will help one stand out in the memory of their conversation partner.

Paraphrasing as a means of making someone remember one for a lifetime is also a way through which one can share their own opinions or viewpoints on varied subjects of interest to their conversation partner.

Questions can be presented in the form of paraphrasing with the focus of engaging one's conversation partner. Letting one's conversation partner expound more on their subject of interest via the use of, e.g. open-ended questions can help one remember the one who was listening as quite a number of people feel good about conversations whereby they were able to give more detail about topics of interest by one who was actively listening to them. To be able to use the tool of questioning well in the form of paraphrasing, it is important for one to focus on what is of interest in the subject matter being discussed.

Point out similarities: To connect with someone at a deep level, it is good to point out what one has in common with the speaker, to the speaker. Doing this creates a bond. Pointing out what is common with someone can help one have influence over another. This assists in scenarios that require persuasion. Pointing similarities out can also help one seem relatable to their conversation partner.

One should point out similarities at appropriate times when the conversation partner pauses. When pointing out similarities, one should endeavor to make the conversation about both parties and not shift the focus of the conversation to themselves.

When pointing out similarities, one can bring in humor to make the feedback interesting. One, though, should be careful to take into note the context within which the conversation is taking place so that one does not end up instead e.g. insulting their conversation partner, even unknowingly. Doing so would leave a negative memory in the mind of one's conversation partner. Humor can also be used as a means to evoke the emotion of joy in one's dialogue partner, which will make one memorable as this is a positive emotion brought out. Individuals generally remember moments or people who make them happy or bring them a feeling of pleasure. Making someone happy can make them feel as though one understands them and accepts them for who they truly are.

Pointing out similarities with one's dialogue partner also showcases one's vulnerability which one's conversation partner can take as an indication of trust, an emotion needed to create positive lifetime bonds.

Pointing out similarities can also be done from the point of complimenting one's dialogue partner. This evokes positive emotions in them, for example, feeling as being considered as one of value. The way to make compliments authentic, so as not to portray one as being a fraud, is to base them on actual accomplishments achieved by the other party. Bringing out one's compliments in an authentic manner leaves them with a good feeling that makes one memorable in the mind of the one complimented. Being specific in compliments evokes stronger emotions than one giving a compliment that is general. The stronger the emotions evoked, the more likely one is to be memorable to the one feeling the emotions. Compliments have the added ability to create an environment that is friendly.

One can also use the tool of pointing out similarities by comparing one's experience with something or an event that is commonly relatable as this can create a mental picture in the mind of one's dialogue partner which can lead to one being memorable. One should be aware, though, that whatever one relates can determine the mental picture created in the minds of their dialogue partners. Whatever one chooses to compare with that is easily relatable should not compete but augment their own actual experience.

Focus on emotion: To connect better, one should focus on understanding the emotion that underlies why someone does something or feels a certain way. Getting to the core of the emotions of the one being listened to creates a bond that lasts. Focusing on emotion in this way leaves an impression on one's dialogue partner. The one thing to remember, though, is one should not make their dialogue partner remember them through the lens of negative emotions.

Focusing on emotion as a tool that can be used to become memorable can mean aiming to make someone feel emotions that are positive when they come into contact with an individual. This can be achieved through offering one's dialogue partner compliments. The focus here should be to offer compliments that are authentic. Offering compliments that are not genuine will create a negative impression. One might feel as though they are being patronized.

One should aim to truly care for the message being shared by their conversation partner and for their dialogue partner as an individual.

As risky as it may seem, one can opt to discuss topics that are considered controversial. Such subject matters, depending on the context within which dialogue is taking place, can result in being remembered positively, particularly if the conversation takes place within the boundaries of mutual respect. One should not confuse controversy for inappropriateness, as the latter will leave a negative impression with the one's dialogue partner and may even lead to loss of respect in their eyes. When bringing up controversial topics, one should be ready to share their reasons why they hold certain viewpoints respectfully. The key here is one should be able to defend their opinions in a tactful manner. Standing apart from the rest via controversy is sometimes not necessarily a negative thing.

Confidence is an emotion that helps in one having a positive impression on someone else for a long time. Individuals generally like being around those who are sure of themselves. Confidence also allows one to interact with a myriad of people as opposed to not interacting with anyone. Confidence can be showcased both verbally and non-verbally. For one to become confident, one should work on being self-aware. In this context, self-awareness should be for the purpose of turning one's weakness into strengths.

In the context of focusing on emotions, one should always aim to focus on emotions that are positive in nature in order to become memorable. People generally do not want to remember negative emotions whilst they love to remember positive ones. It only makes sense, therefore, to focus on associating with emotions that people love to remember as a means of one being remembered for a long time.

Being generous is a way through which one can focus on positive emotion generation, particularly if it is done without expecting anything in return. Generosity should focus on providing something of value to one's dialogue partner. One should remember that generosity is not necessarily giving something tangible like a gift but can be one's time or labor. Generosity focuses on sorting out a challenge for someone else. Introducing someone to an individual who can be of help to them is an example of how one can be generous. One should always remember that generosity is focused on the other individual. One can learn how to tailor a generous act by reading the non-verbal cues in a conversation with a dialogue partner. Generosity as a tool to be memorable does not necessarily have to be direct in nature. One can instead create a situation that will solve the challenges another party is facing. Generosity, in its basic definition, focuses on linking needs with solutions. Generosity leads to the development of relationships which, when worked on further, can grow stronger. When it comes to being generous as a tool to be memorable, one must stay within the boundaries of appropriateness.

To focus on emotions, one can get involved in supporting a charity event. This is an opportunity to meet and bond with like-minded individuals who have a passion for similar causes. The passion they feel for the causes will make those who participate with them in pursuing their passions memorable.

Another way of connecting with emotions that are positive is to willing oneself not to be the one to share their good deeds. When someone else speaks highly of an individual, as opposed to the particular individual shouting out their achievements, the individual evokes a positive memory in those who hear of their good deeds. Using the latter route can be perceived as being boastful and can, therefore, have a negative effect on the kind of memories it evokes, if at all. The focus here for an individual to be memorable in a positive light is to continue with positive actions as opposed to speaking of their positive actions.

In regard to focusing on emotions as a tool that one can use to be memorable, one should always embrace enthusiasm. But of course, this is dependent on the context within which communication is taking place. But enthusiasm is the correct emotion to showcase when meeting people. This helps both parties to be relaxed and changes the mindset to one that is more positive. This can create pleasant memories in one's mind.

A technique called mirroring whereby one reflects the emotions and or gestures of their dialogue partner, but in a subtle manner, can be used as a way for one to be memorable. This technique works at a subconscious level.

Let tension be: When it feels like there is awkwardness when one reveals their vulnerability, one may be tempted to diffuse the situation. The trick here is not to give in to the temptation. Letting the tension allows the speaker to express themselves fully.

Also, for the individual looking to be memorable, let the tension one feels when they try out new ways of improving their memorability be an accepted part of the journey. This will deal with the fear and anxiety that trying out new things can bring. For one to be memorable, they have to be willing to make mistakes even in the public's eyes. Being open to failure can be the very thing that makes one memorable in the other person's mind.

Validation: To create better connections through active listening, a tool that is of use is that of validating the vulnerabilities one exposes to the listener. This can be done by taking part in the emotions that the speaker displays. Being part of the emotional journey gives the one being listened to actively, a feeling of being supported and understood.

Be open: It is important to be vulnerable too as a means of creating a bond that lasts with people. When one shows their vulnerability as a listener, the speaker feels safe sharing their vulnerabilities, too. One, though, should know the boundaries within which vulnerabilities should be shared as one does not want to appear to be sharing too much inappropriately. Also, one should take into consideration the context within which it is okay to share varied types of vulnerabilities. Vulnerability, though, should be authentic as one's dialogue partner will possibly be offended if they were to find out that one shared a supposed vulnerability that in reality, does not even exist. When one is not authentic, they can end up not being memorable. Being self-aware will help one determine when it is the right time to be vulnerable, in what setting and to what extent so that it is portrayed appropriately.

Being open as a tool that can be used to be memorable can mean being open to sharing one's ideas with others. Doing so may end up solving a challenge that someone was experiencing, which in turn will make them remember you for being the source of their solution. The focus here should be the sharing of ideas that can be beneficial in nature, preferably to both parties conversing.

Being open also means being willing to try out new adventures and/or things in life. This will allow one to meet new people, therefore, increasing the richness of their social networks. When one is known across varied networks, they in most cases become memorable as their name will probably pop up more often than not. In addition, trying out new things can help one gather new skills to add on to their skillset, which can make them more valuable to work or associate with. The main goal here is to get more varied experiences. Such experiences can be useful in keeping conversations going with dialogue partners. People also tend to bond better in scenarios that are more relaxing like when taking a hike as this is an experience for them too, which can make one memorable as partners will attach the memory of the experience to the ones whom they shared the experience with.

Being open as a tool of being memorable can be about one opening up about what gave them the inspiration to make certain decisions that changed the course of their lives. Quite a number of those interviewed, are interviewed from this point of view. This is because individuals are generally drawn to stories of inspiration. Individuals are drawn to turning points in people's lives as it can sometimes give hope for a better tomorrow in their own individual lives.

One should be open to every chance of conversing as a possible opportunity to being memorable. Having this mindset will make one relax whilst giving the vibe of the individual being confident, which is an attractive feature that makes one memorable.

To be memorable, one should be open to hearing other points of view on varied subjects even though they may not necessarily hold similar views. This will give one a reputation of being non-judgmental, which is an attractive trait that can make one stand out in one's memory.

The main consideration when looking to create bonds that will make people remember one for a lifetime is remembering to make others feel as being of value. One's attention should be fully on the speaker for effective active listening to occur. Doing this gives one the feeling of having been heard and understood.

Being open also means being able to be honest. People generally appreciate honesty, particularly if shared in a respectful manner without feeling the need to look down on others who may have varied views from one's own. Honesty is generally refreshing in a conversation and may make one memorable, particularly in the world of today where it is hard to come across this characteristic. One should not confuse being honest with being critical or judgmental as the latter two characteristics can make one memorable in a negative sense.

One should always remember that even as one practice to becoming memorable, they are bound to make mistakes, and even in some instances create impressions they did not want to. It is a normal process in the journey of becoming memorable. It is okay always to aim to become a better version of oneself, yet there are times when one has no control over variables that determine how others will remember them.

Working on being memorable can be an important asset in almost all industries and can be what makes one be chosen in the marketplace over another individual. One should remember that being memorable is in many cases, equal to being known. As one works on being memorable, they are more likely to live lives that are more fulfilling. One should remember that being memorable is not necessarily equal to sharing opinions but instead the ability to pull others into having a rich conversation experience.

AFTERWORD

Having read through the book the next step is to make a decision to practice the tips shared in the book. The way to improve any skill is to incorporate practicing its use in everyday life.

One can lookout for opportunities to incorporate some ideas shared in the book. One could also opt to actively recruit close friends or colleagues to help in one's journey to bettering their active listening skills. This can help one get feedback on how they are progressing in their journey to better listening skills.

It is expected that as one follows the guidelines shared, one will become more comfortable and confident in their ability to incorporate the guidelines. The end goal is for the ideas and guidelines shared to be second nature for anyone who makes the decision to embark on this journey of self-development.

The tips and guidelines shared in this book can be implemented in a stepwise manner for easy follow up on progress. The guidelines can be used by both individuals and groups. The tips work in both social and professional contexts. One can also break the tips down to a level that children can be trained on the same.

The guidelines shared therein are precious listening tips, and the reader should be proud daily of the results and change in lifestyle that following the tips and guidelines in this book leads to.

Made in the USA
San Bernardino, CA
23 July 2020